Poverty and home ownership in contemporary Britain

Roger Burrows

The POLICY PRESS

First published in Great Britain in January 2003 by

The Policy Press
34 Tyndall's Park Road
Bristol BS8 1PY
UK

Tel no   +44 (0)117 954 6800
Fax no   +44 (0)117 973 7308
E-mail   tpp-info@bristol.ac.uk
www.policypress.org.uk

Published for the Joseph Rowntree Foundation by The Policy Press

ISBN 1 86134 465 1

Roger Burrows is Professor of Social Policy and Co-Director of the Centre for Housing Policy, University of York.

The **Joseph Rowntree Foundation** has supported this project as part of its programme of research and innovative development projects, which it hopes will be of value to policy makers, practitioners and service users. The facts presented and views expressed in this report are, however, those of the author and not necessarily those of the Foundation.

Photograph on front cover supplied by www.third-avenue.co.uk
Cover design by Qube Design Associates, Bristol
Printed in Great Britain by Hobbs the Printers Ltd, Southampton

Contents

List of tables and figures

Tables

Figures

Acknowledgements

This research would not have been possible without the support of the Joseph Rowntree Foundation. Not only did they fund the project on which this report is based, they also provided the substantial funding necessary for the collection of the data utilised in the report – the Poverty and Social Exclusion (PSE) Survey of Britain. I would particularly like to thank Theresa McDonagh at the Foundation for her understanding, help and enthusiasm.

I would like to thank the following colleagues at the University of York for their extensive help and support: Janet Ford, Steve Wilcox, Jonathan Bradshaw, Naomi Finch, Peter Kemp, Julie Williams and Sarah Nettleton.

Preface

In general, home ownership and poverty have rarely been linked together. The prevailing, popular view of owner occupation is one that associates the tenure with the middle class and more affluent households. In many minds the tenure remains associated with investment and accumulation, and, for these and other reasons, home ownership is still most people's aspiration.

In some respects, these views of home ownership as an affluent, middle-class tenure are well founded. The majority of owner occupiers (those with a mortgage and outright owners) belong to the professional, managerial and intermediate non-manual groups – 60% in 1980 and 62% in 1998. The average gross weekly household income of all owners in 1998 was £555 compared to £203 among local authority tenants (Wilcox, 2000). These figures, however, conceal the diversity of the tenure even though this diversity has long been recognised by housing researchers (Karn, 1979; Forrest et al, 1990). One aspect of this diversity is low-income home ownership. A study of home owners in Birmingham in 1979 was one of the first to draw attention to this development (Karn, 1979), while studies in the late 1980s and early 1990s noted the incidence of unemployment, home ownership and poverty (Ford and Wilcox, 1992; Davis and Dhooge, 1993). It is only recently, however, that there has been a more systematic consideration of the extent of poverty and home ownership.

In *Half the poor: Home owners with low incomes*, Burrows and Wilcox (2000) suggested that 12% of home owners were poor. More strikingly, they also noted that, from the point of view of those who could be defined as poor (using the measure of households below average income), half of these households owned or were buying their own homes. Further, the proportion of the poor who are home owners has grown rapidly since 1979. Among the lowest income decile (measured before housing costs are taken into account), home ownership grew by 18 percentage points to 57% between 1979 and 1997/98, yet the dominance of home ownership within society can make these developments and their implications difficult to recognise.

The growth of home ownership among poor households is connected, in part, with the policy to expand home ownership that accelerated particularly after 1979. The development of mass home ownership (the term 'mature' home ownership is sometimes used) was built on a series of policy interventions which created the fiscal and regulatory structures to support easier access, implemented policies allowing tenants to become owners by buying their previously rented properties, and limited the provision of social housing, particularly local authority housing. So, for example, the financial services sector was deregulated in 1984, creating a highly competitive market in which lenders vied for borrowers in contrast to a previous climate of mortgage rationing. Since 1979, over 1.8 million homes have been bought under the Right-to-Buy and other initiatives, and a proportion of these sales were to the lowest income group, although they were not the predominant beneficiaries. All of these policy initiatives resonated with households' aspirations and, to different degrees, contributed to the growth of low-income home ownership.

But, if widening access has resulted in an increase in poor home owners, so too has the changed socioeconomic environment that sets the conditions under which households manage their housing costs. There is a growing awareness that home ownership is 'riskier' than it once was as a result of events that undermine the ability to meet mortgage payments. In particular, labour market disruption is more frequent, sometimes resulting in unemployment and sometimes re-employment at a lower wage, and relationship breakdown can result in previous partners living on much lower incomes. These processes create a dynamic that, in a proportion of cases, lead to poverty, typically via mortgage arrears and the ongoing recovery of debt. In 2001, 2% of borrowers were in arrears and a total of 13% reported arrears or difficulties paying, almost two thirds as a result of labour market disruptions of various kinds (SEH, 2001). The extent of employment disruption among mortgagors has been shown using data from the British Household Panel Survey. This noted that 28% of mortgagor heads of household experienced at least one change of employment status between 1991 and 1994 and just over 20% between 1995 and 1998 (Ford et al, 2001). While some of these disruptions do not result in low income a proportion clearly do. Thus, some home owners are poor when they enter the tenure but others become poor as a result of unforeseen events.

There is also *some* coincidence between being a low-income entrant and enhanced risk. This is the case with respect to unemployment where there is a social class gradient. Risk may also be enhanced as a result of the substantial proportion of income that low-income home buyers devote to housing costs. Burrows and Wilcox (2000) suggest that taking the affordability criteria of 25% of income for rent used with the social rented sector, then low-income home buyers' housing costs can be clearly seen to exceed those guidelines by a substantial margin. Given this, the room for adjustment in circumstances of rising interest rates or other unexpected demands on household income is limited. On balance, however, the evidence points to the more significant process – numerically – being that of home owners becoming poor rather than entering as poor

The policy to encourage home ownership, the identification of one in eight home owners who are poor and, among those who are poor, evidence that 50% are home owners, raises some questions about the nature of policy responses to the emergence of low-income home ownership. What support, if any, is and should be available to these households to help them sustain their housing?

Currently, the policy context is one that clearly differentiates between owners and renters, to the disadvantage of owners. Focussing first on *home*

buyers, for those in employment, there is no help with housing costs (however low their income), a position at odds with the payment of Housing Benefit to low-income in-work renters under which, in 1998, 1.4 million such households received assistance with housing costs. Unemployed mortgagors do have access to a state safety net, but this has been eroded over a period that coincides with much of the growth in poor home owners. Currently, mortgagors that qualify for Income Support or Jobseekers Allowance can, after a period of up to 39 weeks, receive help with their mortgage interest costs (ISMI) subject to a number of eligibility criteria. (Support is more immediate for certain categories of borrowers – pensioners, for example.) The period before the commencement of state assistance may be covered by private insurance provision, but the costs of purchase are significant at around £5 per month per £100 covered, and a considerable obstacle to poorer households taking out insurance. A key issue, however, for those who do in time receive ISMI is the inherent 'unemployment trap' or work disincentive associated with the need to obtain employment at a wage that not only covers the income replacement benefit but also allows the mortgage costs to be met in full.

In overall terms, among poor households now split roughly 50/50 between owning and renting, tenant households receive 92% of the state's help with housing costs to low-income households, while owner occupiers receive only 8%. Another way of expressing the inequity is to note that in May 1998, 4.5 million low-income tenants were receiving Housing Benefit but only 335,000 home owners (those with no income other than benefit) were in receipt of assistance with their mortgage costs. These inequities remain, notwithstanding a small number of concessions towards mortgagors returning to employment announced in the 2000 Housing Green Paper (DETR, 2000). ISMI now continues over the first four weeks of work, assisting with return to work costs. In addition, the work disincentive associated with short-term employment has been addressed, increasing the period from 13 to 52 weeks, during which any reapplication for ISMI is not subject to the nine month requalifying period.

Calls to address the inequitable provision to low-income home owners are longstanding. In 1991, there was a proposal calling for a mortgage benefit, following work undertaken by the Joseph Rowntree Housing Inquiry and reinforced by the serious development of arrears and possessions in the early 1990s (Wilcox and Webb, 1991). Similar proposals were contained in a report published by the Council for Mortgage Lenders in 1997 (Wilcox and Sutherland, 1997), while evidence in support of a tenure-neutral housing allowance was placed before the 2000 Social Security Select Committee special enquiry into Housing Benefit, and reiterated in the Burrows and Wilcox (2000) report noted above. The introduction of Working Families' Tax Credit which is payable to both home owners and tenants does, in principle, alleviate the financial position of some low-income owners but, in some circumstances, will not fully match the out-of-work assistance and is not a direct response to housing costs. More recent proposals have sought to gain support for a housing credit, along with some better integration of the range of benefits and credits now available. However, the absence of an in-work mortgage cost-related benefit continues to be a policy deficit both with respect to encouraging and enabling home owners to return to work, and in respect of sustainable home ownership.

This growing focus on home ownership and poverty is important and welcome. The impetus to explore this issue, certainly with respect to discussions of policy, has come, to date, from those primarily concerned with housing. What the report presented here does is to focus on the same issue but starting from a different point. It explores the relationship through a different lens, namely the concept of poverty. A range of conceptualisations and associated measurements of poverty are used to offer a 'vigorous appraisal' of the current claim that half the poor are home owners, based as it is on one particular conceptualisation of poverty, that signified by households below an 'officially' designated income line(s). If, when measured in other ways, similar conclusions about the relationship between poverty and home ownership are reached, the policy implications outlined above gain additional credence. However, widening the approach in this way is not just an opportunity to confirm (or otherwise) a previous claim, it also offers an opportunity to extend the consideration of poverty and home ownership further and, in particular, to enhance our understanding of the nature of poverty among home owners per se in comparison with those in other tenures.

Professor Janet Ford, Centre for Housing Policy,
University of York, May 2002

References

Burrows, R. and Wilcox, S. (2000) *Half the poor: Home owners with low incomes*, London: Council of Mortgage Lenders.

Davis, R. and Dhooge, Y. (1993) *Living with mortgage arrears*, London: HMSO.

DETR (Department for the Environment, Transport and the Regions) (2000) *Housing Green Paper*, London: The Stationery Office.

Ford, J. and Wilcox, S. (1992) *Reducing mortgage arrears and possessions: Evaluating the initiatives*, York: Joseph Rowntree Foundation.

Ford, J., Burrows, R. and Nettleton, S. (2001) *Home ownership in a risk society: A social analysis of mortgage arrears and possession*, Bristol: The Policy Press.

Forrest, R., Murie, A. and Williams, P. (1990) *Home ownership, differentiation and fragmentation*, London: Unwin Hyman.

Karn, V. (1979) 'Low-income owner occupation in the inner city', in C. Jones (ed) *Urban deprivation in the inner city*, London: Croom Helm.

SEH (*Survey of English Housing*) (2001) London: DTLR.

Wilcox, S. (2000) *Housing Finance Review*, Coventry/London/York: Chartered Institute of Housing/Council of Mortgage Lenders/Joseph Rowntree Foundation.

Wilcox, S. and Sutherland, H. (1997) *Securing home ownership: Providing an effective safety-net for home owners*, London: Council of Mortgage Lenders.

Wilcox, S. and Webb, S. (1991) *Time for mortgage benefits*, York: Joseph Rowntree Foundation.

Introduction

In 1945 most people in Britain rented their accommodation. Home ownership accounted for no more than 40% of all households. By 1971 this proportion had increased to just over one half. By 1981 it had increased further to just over 56%. By 1991, a full two thirds of households were home owners. Currently the figure stands at 68% (Wilcox, 2001, p 91). The reasons for this growth in home ownership have been well documented (Hamnett, 1999; Ford et al, 2001). It was evident in the 1970s that there was a long-standing public preference for home ownership, but it was only after a series of policy initiatives that this potential demand was fully realised. The major initiatives were, first, the mandatory selling of social housing at a discounted rate under the Right-to Buy (RTB) scheme, which formed part of the 1980 Housing Act and has to date resulted in the sale of almost 1.93 million dwellings in the social rented sector (Wilcox, 2001, p 100). This policy was accompanied by a second that placed restrictions on the use by the local authorities of the capital receipts from the sale of their property for replacement building. Together, these policies resulted in a reduction of good quality property to rent and led to the residualisation of much of the social rented sector (Forrest and Murie, 1990). The government also acted to deregulate the credit market through the 1985 Financial Services Act and the 1986 Building Societies Act, which encouraged new entrant credit providers. A highly competitive market resulted, in which lenders increasingly offered mortgages to groups who had hitherto been regarded as 'riskier' customers. These initiatives unleashed the mid- and late-1980s housing market boom.

The changes in housing policy over the period not only resulted in an increase in the number of home owners; the growth in home ownership was accompanied by some important changes in the socioeconomic characteristics of home owners. While owner occupation in general, and mortgagors in particular, remain heavily characterised as middle class, home ownership has, in reality, become far more diverse, and arguably now constitutes the most diverse tenure in Britain. Since 1979 there has been a reduction in the proportion of younger borrowers and an increase in older mortgagors; a small increase in the proportion of manual worker mortgagors and a significant increase in economically inactive mortgagors. The proportion of households from minority ethnic groups has also increased although not uniformly. The consequences of these changes in the socioeconomic profile of the tenure are complex (Ford et al, 2001), but one fundamental outcome has been that an increasing proportion of home owners are poor.

A recent exploratory study (Burrows and Wilcox, 2000), drawing on a range of secondary analyses of official data sources, has suggested that at least *one half* all households living in poverty are home owners. The contention that home owners now form half of the poor in Britain – if it is true has implications at a number of levels. At a theoretical level it requires us to rethink our conceptual map of the social distribution of poverty, not least in the way in which housing tenure is sometimes used as a measure of relative dis/advantage (Smith et al, 2002). It also means that some of the very real risks associated with home ownership need to be more fully incorporated within the poverty research literature, especially perhaps those aspects relating to health (Nettleton and Burrows, 2000) and family life (Nettleton and Burrows, 2001). At the policy level it demands that we reassess the equity of current state help with housing costs. If home owners do indeed form half of the poor we must begin to ask if it is equitable that they currently only receive 8% of the state help with housing costs targeted on low income households (Burrows et al, 2000). Also, we might need to question further the efficacy of area-based interventions aimed to alleviate poverty, which are generally targeted at locations dominated by social housing. Such policy instruments will generally miss poor home owners (Lee and Murie, 1997; Burrows and Rhodes, 2000) who, for the most part, are not concentrated within particular neighbourhoods in the same way as households living in the social rented sector.

In this report the contention that home owners in Britain now constitute half the poor is subject to a vigorous appraisal using a data source expressly designed for the purpose of measuring poverty and social exclusion – the Joseph Rowntree Foundation Poverty and Social Exclusion (PSE) Survey of Britain (Gordon et al, 2000). Use of this data set has a distinct advantage over the range of different official data sources utilised by Burrows and Wilcox (2000) in their review of the available evidence on home ownership and poverty. All of the official data sources used by Burrows and Wilcox rely, albeit in different ways, on a conceptualisation of poverty that assumes people to be in poverty if they have incomes below an arbitrary percentage of average incomes (for example, below half average income or incomes in the bottom quintile of the income distribution). Such an approach to the estimation of poverty has been criticized by Gordon et al because, although it

is convenient ... it is not scientifically based: that is, it is not based on independent criteria of deprivation or disadvantage; it does not relate to the needs of individuals, or to any agreed definition of what it is to be poor. (2000, pp 8-9)

In this report data from the PSE Survey is used in order to operationalise the concept of poverty in three different ways. This is done in order to examine whether the conclusions one comes to regarding the extent and nature of poverty among home owners is a function of the definition of poverty used. Chapter 2 provides some details about the PSE Survey and Chapter 3 discusses the operationalisation of each of the three conceptualisations of poverty, while Chapter 4 examines the relationship between

each of our three measures of poverty and housing tenure. Chapters 5 to 8 are taken up with a detailed examination of the nature and extent of poverty among home owners in comparison with people living in poverty in other tenures.

The Poverty and Social Exclusion Survey of Britain

There were two parts to the PSE Survey. First, a representative sample of the population of Britain were asked for their views on what constitute the necessities of life in present day Britain that no household or family should be without. This was undertaken by the Office of National Statistics (ONS) in June 1999 as part of an Omnibus Survey. A sample of 3,000 addresses was selected from the Postcode Address File (PAF) and within each address one person aged 16 or over was randomly selected and interviewed face-to-face. In total, 1,855 interviews were achieved. From this data it was possible to derive a listing of perceptions of adult necessities; where more than one half of the population thought something was necessary it was included in the list of necessities. So, to take a few examples, 95% of people considered beds and bedding for everyone in the household to be a necessity, 91% considered two meals a day to be a necessity and 76% considered a washing machine to be a necessity. At the other end of the scale just 6% thought that access to the Internet should be regarded as a necessity and only 7% thought that ownership of a mobile 'phone was a necessity. A full list of the items that people were asked to consider is shown in Table 1 (overleaf).

The second part of the PSE Survey was as a follow up to the 1998/99 General Household Survey (GHS) (full details of the study design can be found in Appendix 4 of Gordon et al, 2000). Data from the 1998/99 GHS were used in order to select a sample of individuals for the PSE Survey with known characteristics. A total of 1,534 interviews were achieved. The fieldwork was carried out in September and October 1999. Background demographic, socioeconomic and income data on the respondents had already been collected as part of the GHS and the PSE

Survey collected data on ownership of socially perceived necessities (as derived from the Omnibus Survey described above), housing, health, social support, debts, area deprivation, local services, crime, schooling, political activism and a host of other topics. The data was weighted in order to make the final sample as representative of the adult population in Britain as possible[1].

---

[1] The PSE data file used in this report is one that has been updated since the publication of Gordon et al (2000). A range of improvements have been made to the data following extensive checks of data quality carried out by the PSE Survey research team.

Table 1: Perception of adult necessities and how many people lack them (% of adult population)

		Omnibus Survey: items considered	Main stage survey: items that respondents	
Items considered for inclusion in deprivation scale including notes on final validity, reliability and additivity of each item[a]		Necessary	Don't have because they don't want	Don't have, because they can't afford
1	Beds and bedding for everyone [not valid or reliable]	95	0	1
2	Heating to warm living areas of the home	94	0	1
3	Damp-free home	93	3	6
4	Visiting friends or family in hospital	92	8	3
5	Two meals a day	91	3	1
6	Medicines prescribed by doctor [not additive]	90	5	1
7	Refrigerator [not valid or reliable]	89	1	0
8	Fresh fruit and vegetables daily	86	7	4
9	Warm, waterproof coat	85	2	4
10	Replace or repair broken electrical goods	85	6	12
11	Visits to friends or family	84	3	2
12	Celebrations on special occasions such as Christmas	83	2	2
13	Money to keep home in decent state of decoration	82	2	14
14	Visits to school, such as sports day	81	33	2
15	Attending weddings, funerals	80	3	3
16	Meat, fish or vegetarian equivalent every other day	79	4	3
17	Insurance of contents of dwelling	79	5	8
18	Hobby or leisure activity	78	12	7
19	Washing machine [not valid or reliable]	76	3	1
20	Collect children from school	75	36	2
21	Telephone	71	1	1
22	Appropriate clothes for job interviews	69	13	4
23	Deep freezer/fridge freezer [not additive]	68	3	2
24	Carpets in living rooms and bedrooms	67	2	3
25	Regular savings (of £10 per month) for rainy days	66	7	25
26	Two pairs of all-weather shoes	64	4	5
27	Friends or family round for a meal	64	10	6
28	A small amount of money to spend on self weekly, not on family	59	3	13
29	Television [not valid or reliable]	56	1	1
30	Roast joint/vegetarian equivalent once a week	56	11	3
31	Presents for friends/family once a year	56	1	3
32	Holiday away from home once a year, not staying with relatives	55	14	18
33	Replace worn out furniture	54	6	12
34	Dictionary	53	6	5
35	An outfit for social occasions	51	4	4
36	*New, not second-hand, clothes*	*48*	*4*	*5*
37	*Attending place of worship*	*42*	*65*	*1*
38	*Car*	*38*	*12*	*10*
39	*Coach/train fares to visit friends/family quarterly*	*38*	*49*	*16*
40	*An evening out once a fortnight*	*37*	*22*	*15*
41	*Dressing gown*	*34*	*12*	*6*
42	*Having a daily newspaper*	*30*	*37*	*4*
43	*A meal in a restaurant/pub monthly*	*26*	*20*	*18*
44	*Microwave oven*	*23*	*16*	*3*
45	*Tumble dryer*	*20*	*33*	*7*
46	*Going to the pub once a fortnight*	*20*	*42*	*10*

Table 1: contd.../

Items considered for inclusion in deprivation scale including notes on final validity, reliability and additivity of each item[a]	Omnibus Survey: items considered	Main stage survey: items that respondents	
	Necessary	Don't have because they don't want	Don't have, because they can't afford
47 *Video cassette recorder*	19	7	2
48 *Holidays abroad once a year*	19	25	27
49 *CD player*	12	19	7
50 *Home computer*	11	42	15
51 *Dishwasher*	7	57	11
52 *Mobile 'phone*	7	48	7
53 *Access to the Internet*	6	54	16
54 *Satellite television*	5	56	7

Note: [a]Items shown in italics <50% considered as necessities so not considered in final scale construction.

3

Measuring poverty

The data collected for the PSE Survey can be used to measure poverty in a number of different ways. Here we consider three rather different approaches. First, a simple measure of poverty as low income, similar to that used in the various data sources utilised in Burrows and Wilcox (2000); second, that developed by the PSE Survey team (Gordon et al, 2000, pp 7-31); and, third, a 'needs'-based approach recently advocated by Bradshaw and Finch (2001) in their attempt to identify what they term *core* or *real* poverty. Together these three conceptualisations cover a very broad range of different approaches to the study of poverty. In this section we outline each approach in turn, beginning with the most simple (poverty measured on one domain – income) and ending with the most complex (the Bradshaw and Finch conceptualisation of poverty measured on four domains).

The low household income approach to measuring poverty

The PSE Survey contains data on both gross and net household income for 90% of adults in the sample. This data has been equivalised using the standard McClements equivalence scale as used by the ONS. This data can be used in a number of different ways to define poverty. We could define it (as is commonly done) as half the mean average income or some other proportion of mean average income. However, we have decided to define it in terms of those with incomes in the bottom 20% of the income distribution. Equivalised income has thus been grouped into quintiles, with the bottom quintile comprising households with the lowest incomes and the top quintile those households with the highest incomes. This gives a measure of

household income 'before housing costs' (BHC) as the General Household Survey does not contain sufficient information to construct an 'after housing costs' (AHC) measure[2]. For our purposes we shall define adults to be in poverty on this measure if they live *within households who are in the bottom quintile of equivalised net income before housing costs*. By definition this means that 20% of people are in poverty.

The PSE Survey approach to measuring poverty

The PSE Survey approach to poverty is based on a consideration of the relationship between levels of deprivation and levels of income. Levels of deprivation were measured using the data collected on socially perceived necessities.

[2] Differences in BHC and AHC incomes are important when analysing differences across housing tenures, but in this analysis we are restricted to using a BHC measure only. In general the AHC measure used in official statistics does not take account of home owners' expenditure on repairs and maintenance. In contrast, these items are covered by rental payments. Moreover, it should also be noted that, for home buyers with mortgages, housing costs include mortgage interest payments but not capital repayments. Even if the view is taken that capital repayments should be excluded (even though payment is unavoidable), the inclusion of repair costs alone within the definition of housing costs would itself result in an appreciable increase in the numbers of low-income home owners in any AHC analyses. Thus, although an AHC analysis might estimate there to be a smaller proportion of poor home owners than a BHC analysis suggests, this would, in reality, be an underestimate. Under such circumstances a BHC analysis, such as that to be undertaken here, may not be as problematic as it first appears.

Only the 35 items that 50% or more of the population stated they perceived to be a necessity were included in the analysis (see Table 1). These items were used to construct an index of deprivation based on whether respondents stated that they 'did not have because they could not afford'. The reliability, validity and additivity of each item in the index was then tested (see Gordon et al, 2000, pp 77-9). It was discovered that four of the items – a television, a refrigerator, beds and bedding for everyone and a washing machine – were either not valid or unreliable items, and that a further two – medicines prescribed by a doctor and a deep-freezer/fridge-freezer – were not additive. These six items were thus dropped from the final deprivation scale. Statistical techniques (logistic regression and ANOVA) were then used in combination with income data in order to determine a 'poverty threshold' (the deprivation score that maximises the 'between group' differences and minimises the 'within group' differences). Both approaches reached the same conclusion – that an optimal poverty threshold occurs at the point at which there is an enforced lack of any two of the 29 necessities.

On this basis, people could be considered to be in poverty if there were at least two socially defined necessities which they were unable to afford. However, two further considerations are necessary given the empirical relationship between the deprivation scale and income. First, some were unable to afford two necessities but had relatively high incomes – these people were classified as having recently *risen out of poverty* (for example, they may have recently gained employment following a period of unemployment). Second, some people did not lack two or more necessities but had relatively low incomes – these people were classified as being *vulnerable to poverty* (for example, they may recently have lost a job but had not yet lost some of the items perceived to be necessities of life).

Using the PSE Survey approach to the conceptualisation of poverty at the end of the 20th century it is estimated that:

- 25% of the adult population of Britain were living in poverty;
- 2% were rising out of poverty;
- 12% were potentially vulnerable to poverty;
- 61% were not living in poverty.

The Bradshaw and Finch approach to measuring poverty

Bradshaw and Finch (2001) have recently used the PSE Survey data to attempt to identify something that might be called *core* or *real* poverty in Britain. This alternative approach to the conceptualisation of poverty is based on a rearticulation of some of the ideas which underpinned the *taxonomy of social need* developed by Bradshaw in the early 1970s (Bradshaw, 1972). In radical contradistinction to constructivist and postmodern tendencies in contemporary social policy discourses (Carter, 1998; Petersen et al, 1999), Bradshaw argues for the existence of ontologically intransitive *real needs*, which are, in turn, the product of some combination of four different types of need: *normative* need, *felt* need, *expressed* need and *comparative* need. Within this conceptualisation *normative* need refers to a lack of socially perceived necessities, *felt* need simply refers to those who say that they feel poor, *expressed* need refers to felt poverty translated into a demand that may or may not be met, and *comparative* need refers to those with limited financial resources relative to other people in their society. For Bradshaw, these four elements of need overlap, and somewhere in the region of the overlap real need can be found. Where real need is found one will also find *real* or *core* poverty. This is shown diagrammatically in Figure 1.

Bradshaw and Finch (2001) use the PSE Survey data in order to operationalise each of these different types of need.

- *Normative* need is operationalised as lacking four or more items identified as necessities by more than half the adult population in the ONS Omnibus Survey (as detailed in Table 1). Using this measure the PSE Survey estimates that 17% of people are in normative need.
- *Felt* need is operationalised as follows. Respondents are first asked: 'How many pounds a week, after tax, do you think are necessary to keep a household such as the one you live in, out of poverty?' They are then asked: 'How far above or below that level would you say your household is?' They can reply that they are either: 'a lot above that level of income'; 'a little above'; 'about the same'; 'a little below'; or 'a lot below that level

Figure 1: Conceptual relationship between the taxonomy of need and real or core poverty

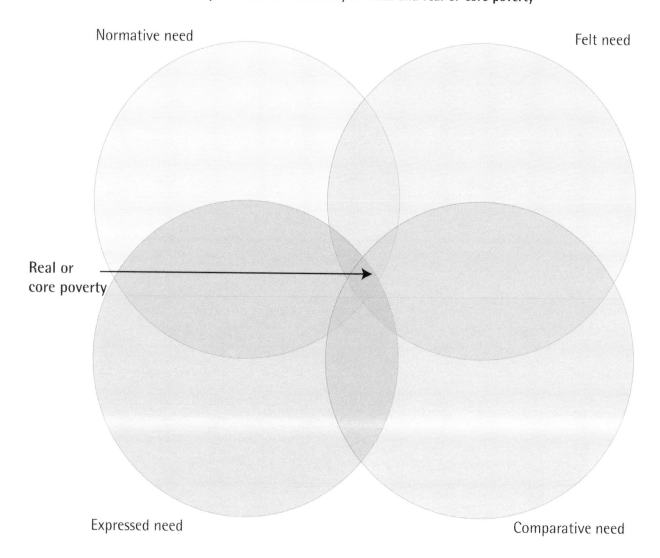

Normative need

Felt need

Real or
core poverty

Expressed need

Comparative need

of income'. Those who respond that they are either 'a little below' or 'a lot below that level of income' are considered to be in this type of need. Using this measure the PSE Survey estimates that 20% of people are in felt need.

- *Expressed* need is operationalised as those receiving Income Support or income-tested Jobseeker's Allowance (IS/JSA). This is recognised by Bradshaw and Finch (2001) as a crude measure for at least two reasons. First, it does not include those who had expressed a need unsuccessfully. Second, ideally such a measure should include those receiving any of the means-tested benefits (Family Credit, Housing Benefit/Council Tax Benefit, Disabled Working Allowance and so on) but data on receipt of these is not available in the General Household Survey. Of course, receipt of the means-tested benefits are not the only social security benefits that demonstrate an expressed need – even contributory benefits and non-contributory non-means-tested

benefits require an individual to make a claim. However, Bradshaw and Finch suggest that those expressing a need for means-tested benefits are perhaps expressing a more urgent need. Using this measure the PSE Survey estimates that 8% of people are in expressed need.

- *Comparative* need is operationalised as those households with net equivalent household income less than 60% of the median before housing costs, using a modified OECD scale. Using this measure the PSE Survey estimates that 19% of people are in this type of need.

The set of analytic distinctions between different types of need developed by Bradshaw and Finch is appealing. This is an approach based on the development of a set of conceptual distinctions, which have a firm philosophical basis and which have been made much use of in a wide range of social policy discourses (Bradshaw, 1994). It is also an approach that includes a wide set of different attributes – material differences, subjective feelings, human actions and the impact of social relativities – within a consistent analytic framework. However, one of the difficulties with the Bradshaw and Finch approach is that in drawing on a number of different dimensions (all of which in and of themselves must be considered entirely valid indicators of poverty), the conceptual and operational amalgam that results is not one which is perfectly fused. Indeed, such is the lack of overlap between the four measures that, if they were completely uncorrelated, one would expect to obtain a distribution very close to the one obtained:

- 34% are in need on at least one dimension;
- 19% are in need on at least two measures;
- 8% are in need on at least three measures; but only
- 3% are in need on all four measures simultaneously.

Of course some lack of overlap is inevitable given the different proportions included by each of the measures used – especially when the analysis includes the smaller percentage on Income Support. However, Bradshaw and Finch also provide a number of other quite plausible reasons, which, in combination, might account for this lack of overlap. First, as explicitly recognised in the PSE Survey measure, there are cases 'in transition' – either about to 'enter' or about to 'leave' poverty. Second, there is 'false consciousness' of various sorts, for example, in the subjective measure, people may claim to be in poverty when they are not (by other dimensions) and people may not feel they are in poverty because they have limited understanding of relative living standards. Third, there are technical explanations to do with the measures themselves. One of these that is likely to be important is the fact that, as we have already noted, the General Household Survey income variable used is BHC. At a given BHC equivalent income level, households with high housing costs are more likely to feel poor and lack social necessities than households with low housing costs. In London, for example, a region with a low income poverty rate, the socially perceived necessities rate is high. This may be due to the impact of high housing costs. Finally, perceptions of poverty may vary according to how resources are distributed *within* the household. Thus, for example, a female non-breadwinner respondent may feel poor because

her breadwinner partner does not share his 'non-poverty' income with her.

One must conclude that there is no easy way to reconcile these different measures of need into a unitary measure of core or real poverty. However, each dimension of need clearly taps into important aspects of what it means to be poor. So, how to proceed? Bradshaw and Finch suggest two possible strategies. First, one could take a *cumulative* approach and consider that a person who is in need on all dimensions is more likely to be in core poverty than a person in need on only one of the dimensions. Further, that being in need on two dimensions is more likely to be core poverty than being in need on one, and less likely than in need on three or four. The more components that define a person as in need the more likely they are to be in core poverty.

Second, one could take what Bradshaw and Finch term a *merit* approach – the idea that one dimension of need has more merit than another and/or that certain combinations of different types of need have more merit than other combinations. So, for example, can a person be defined as poor if s/he does not feel poor? Feeling poor may be a necessary if not a sufficient condition. So anyone who is core poor may have to be poor on the subjective dimension. Another example might be the argument that because lacking four socially perceived necessities is a direct indicator of need it should be given a priority over having a low income which is an indirect and perhaps more imperfect measure of need.

Using all of the four dimensions of need in this way generates 16 different possible combinations. The first combination – in need on all of the four dimensions – unambiguously defines someone as living in *core poverty*. The final combination – not in need on any of the four dimensions – unambiguously defines someone as *not living in poverty*. The merits and demerits of the other 14 combinations for defining poverty obviously vary and all can, to a greater or lesser extent, be contested[3].

---

3   It should be made clear that the use to which the Bradshaw and Finch measure of poverty is being put in this report is entirely the responsibility of the present author.

Table 2: Poverty rates by different permutations of need derived from the Bradshaw and Finch conceptualisation of poverty

	Dimension of need				%	Person in poverty?
	Normative	Felt	Expressed	Comparative		
1	yes	yes	yes	yes	2.5	Core poverty
2	yes	yes	yes	no	1.1	Poverty
3	yes	yes	no	no	4.4	Moderate poverty
4	yes	no	no	no	3.6	Moderate poverty
5	no	yes	yes	yes	0.9	Poverty
6	no	no	yes	yes	1.5	Moderate poverty
7	no	no	no	yes	6.2	Moderate poverty
8	no	yes	no	yes	2.5	Moderate poverty
9	yes	no	yes	no	0.5	Moderate poverty
10	no	yes	yes	no	0.5	Moderate poverty
11	no	no	yes	no	1.1	Moderate poverty
12	yes	no	no	yes	1.1	Moderate poverty
13	yes	yes	no	yes	3.1	Poverty
14	yes	no	yes	yes	0.6	Moderate poverty
15	no	yes	no	no	4.6	Moderate poverty
16	no	no	no	no	66.0	Not in poverty

A strong case can be made for defining anyone who is in need on any three of the dimensions as living in *poverty* (although this assumes, of course, that we treat the four dimensions as if they were all of equal importance). The only ambiguous instance might be those people who are in need on all dimensions except the subjective measure (combination 14). There could be various reasons for this. These people might be students at a stage of life where the lack of items such as carpets is not considered as a mark of poverty; they might be older people with no or little interest in the acquisition of certain otherwise highly popular consumer durables; or they might be people at various stages of the life cycle who might be following what is sometimes termed a 'voluntarily simplistic lifestyle' (Etzioni, 1998), in the sense that their apparent 'poverty' does not translate into a felt need because it is a product of 'choice' rather than something over which they have no control. Nevertheless, this group is clearly still vulnerable and is perhaps best considered to be living in *moderate poverty*.

None of the six categories that define people as being in need on just two dimensions unambiguously define people as being in poverty and, thus, all are perhaps best

considered as being examples of people living in situations which can place them in *moderate poverty*, in the sense that they are vulnerable to changes that could result in the creation of a third type of need, which, would, within this framework, define them as being in poverty.

Finally, none of the combinations in which people are defined as being in need on just one dimension appear to be an adequate basis for defining someone as being in poverty. Such people are, again, living in *moderate poverty* but they are obviously not as vulnerable as people identified as having two types of need.

Table 2 shows all 16 logical permutations of need, the overall poverty rate that each generates and the way in which each category has been reclassified within our much-simplified schema. The large group (over one quarter) classified as being in *moderate poverty* contains people ranged across a wide continuum of need, with some very close to the poverty threshold and some very close to being defined as not being in poverty.

Using our reworking of the Bradshaw and Finch approach to the conceptualisation of poverty at the end of the 20th century we estimate that:

- 3% of the adult population of Britain were living in core poverty;
- 5% were living in poverty;
- 26% were – to a greater or a lesser extent – living in moderate poverty; and
- 66% were not living in poverty.

Relations between the three measures

Our three competing measures of poverty in Britain present us with a choice between:

- a *maximalist* definition (the PSE Survey approach), which defines 25% of the adult population as in poverty;
- an *intermediate* definition (the low household income approach), which defines 20% of the adult population as in poverty;
- a *minimalist* definition (the Bradshaw and Finch approach), which defines 8% of the adult population as in poverty (including those in core poverty) but with a large social hinterland of people living close to the margins of poverty.

Clearly, there is a complex overlap between these three different definitions, as can be seen from Figure 2.

Of the 1,215 people in the sample for which it is possible to operationalise all three of the measures, 66% are defined as not being in poverty on any of the measures. This means, of course, that 34% are defined as being in poverty on one or more of the measures: almost 6% are defined as poor on all three measures; almost 7% are defined as poor by a combination of any two of the measures; and over 21% are defined as poor by only one of the measures. Of people defined as poor by the minimalist measure, 93% are also defined as such by the maximalist measure. However, overall, it is clear that who is and who is not defined as poor is strongly influenced by the nature of the conceptualisation of poverty utilised – poverty is clearly 'concept dependent' (Sayer, 1984, pp 32-5).

Figure 2: Overlap between the three different measures of poverty

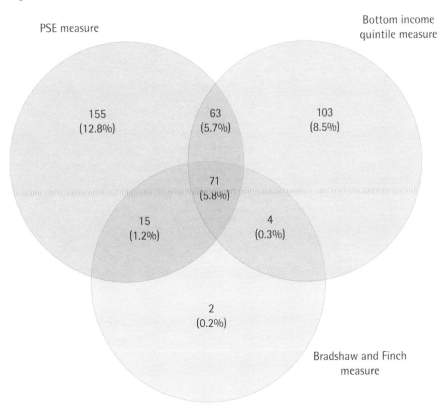

4

The sociodemographic correlates of poverty

As might be expected, the sociodemographic characteristics of the people who are defined as poor differ somewhat across the three measures. Tables 3, 4 and 5 show how rates of poverty vary for each of the three different measures across the categories of nine common sociodemographic variables – housing tenure, the social class of the head of household, the number of workers in the household, age, the region in which the person lives, ethnicity, the type of household the person lives in, gender and current marital status. The tables also show which of these variables, acting in combination, best predict that someone will be in poverty. The variables have been ranked in each table in order to reflect the relative importance of each in accounting for the variation in the odds that a person will be in poverty (measured by a statistic that indicates the change in the log-likelihood ratio).

The first column of each table shows the variable being examined. If there exists significant statistical variation in the rates of poverty across the categories of the variable this is indicated (* <0.05; ** <0.01; and *** <0.001). The second column of each table details how the poverty rate actually varies across the categories of each variable. The third column shows what percentage of those in poverty are in each of these categories. The fourth column shows the base numbers used in order to calculate the rates shown in the second and third columns. The final column shows the results of a logistic regression analysis to predict the odds of poverty using all nine of the variables in each of the tables. The level of significance of each variable in the model is indicated (+ <0.05; ++ <0.01; and +++ <0.001), as is the change in a statistic called the log-likelihood ratio ($\triangle$LLR), which gives an indication of the relative importance of each

variable in the model in explaining the overall variation in the odds. Within each variable the relative impact on the odds of being in one category rather than another after the influence of all of the other variables in the model have been allowed for has been calculated ('the adjusted odds'), and where this is statically significant this is indicated (* <0.05; ** <0.01; and *** <0.001). These odds ratios have been calculated in relation to either a particular reference category (set at 1.0) or to the overall mean effect of the variable (which has been set at 1.0), whichever is the most appropriate given the particular nature of each variable.

The PSE measure of poverty

Consider, as an illustrative example, the variable that is the prime focus of this report – housing tenure. In Table 3 this variable has been categorised into four: those who are outright owners; those who are buying their accommodation with a mortgage; those who live in the social housing sector (accommodation rented from either a local authority [LA] or a registered social landlord [RSL]); and those who live in the private rented sector (PRS). The *** against the tenure variable signifies that variation in the overall poverty rate across these four categories is significantly different at p<0.001. The details of this variation can be seen in the second column. Among outright owners only 15% are defined as poor by the PSE poverty measure, and among those buying with a mortgage just 17% are defined as such. However, among those living in the PRS over one third (34%) are defined as living in poverty and in the social rented sector 61% are defined as such. The third column shows the tenure

Table 3: PSE poverty measure sociodemographics

Variable	% in poverty	% of poor	Number	Adjusted odds
All	25	100	1,534	
Tenure***				+++[△LLR 51.7]
Owned outright	15	18	447	0.6***
Buying with a mortgage	17	32	724	0.6**
Social housing	61	41	263	2.4***
Private rented sector	34	9	97	1.1
Social class of head of household***				+++[△LLR 50.6]
I	3	1	135	0.2***
II	13	14	405	0.6**
IIIN	25	16	235	1.1
IIIM	29	32	411	1.3
IV	43	27	234	2.2***
V	44	8	64	1.9*
Students	50	4	28	0.8
Army	33	0	[3]	2.1
Number of workers in household***				+++[△LLR 46.7]
0	37	50	519	1
1	25	25	374	0.4***
2	14	18	505	0.2***
3	24	7	118	0.2***
4	6	0	[18]	0.1***
Age***				+++[△LLR 37.4]
16-24	34	11	126	1.4
25-34	36	27	286	2.5***
35-44	21	14	259	1.1
45-54	24	16	254	1.6**
55-64	20	14	260	0.9
65-74	20	10	195	0.5**
75+	21	9	154	0.3***
Region**				+++[△LLR 23.2]
North	23	21	362	0.7
Midlands	20	23	279	1.7*
South	18	27	484	1.1
London	18	11	155	1.3
Wales	17	10	116	1.9**
Scotland	24	8	137	0.8
Ethnicity***				+++[△LLR 21.1]
White	23	89	1,467	1
Black or minority ethnic group	62	11	68	4.6***
Type of household***				+++[△LLR 13.4]
Single person	32	24	293	0.8
Couple with no dependent children	16	20	492	0.5**
Couple with dependent children	23	37	609	0.9
Lone mother	52	16	117	1.1
Lone father	50	2	[14]	1.5
Gay couple	33	1	[9]	1.7
Gender**				+++[△LLR 5.1]
Male	22	42	739	1.0
Female	28	58	796	1.4*
Current marital status***				ns
Single, never married	32	27	328	–
Married	19	44	893	–
Separated	49	5	37	–
Divorced	39	14	138	–
Widowed	27	10	136	–

structure of those defined as being in poverty by the PSE measure. It shows that, although the poverty rate in the owner-occupied sector is far lower than in the other tenures, the relative size of the owner-occupied sector means that a full 50% of those living in poverty are either outright owners (18%) or people paying a mortgage (32%). Just over 40% of those living in poverty live in social housing and just under 10% live in the PRS. On the PSE measure of poverty then, not only are half the poor owner occupiers, but owner-occupation is also the most common tenure of those living in poverty.

The final column of Table 3 shows the influence of housing tenure on the odds that someone will be in poverty on the PSE measure once the influence of all of the other variables has been controlled for. The change in the log-likelihood ratio shows that housing tenure is the most influential factor in determining if someone is in poverty on the PSE measure. This is closely followed by social class of the head of household, the number of workers in the household, age, region, ethnicity, household type and gender. Current marital status has no additional influence on the odds once all of the other variables have been considered. As we would expect, within the tenure variable the odds ratios show that, after controlling for all of the other variables, housing tenure still exerts a strong and significant influence on the odds of someone being in poverty on the PSE measure. Owner occupiers are significantly less likely to be in poverty, and those in social housing are significantly more likely to be in poverty.

Table 3 also shows that the social class of the head of household remains an important determinant of poverty – just 3% of those in social class I are in poverty compared to 44% in social class V. This strong class gradient remains even after the odds of poverty are adjusted to take account of the influence of the other variables.

The number of workers in a household also exerts an important influence on the odds of poverty. Among households with no workers, 37% of people are in poverty – a full 50% of people living in poverty live in households where no one works. This contrasts with households where two people are working in which just 14% of people are in poverty. Again,

this relationship holds even after the influence of the other variables is controlled for.

The age of a person also exerts an independent effect on the odds of poverty. In general it is younger people who are the most likely to be in poverty on this measure and older people who are the least likely. People aged between 25 and 34 are the most likely to be living in poverty.

There also exists some evidence that there are independent regional[4] influences on the odds of living in poverty. After controlling for the influence of all of the other variables, those living in the Midlands and Wales still possess a higher chance of living in poverty on the PSE measure than do people living elsewhere.

On the PSE measure, people who self-identify as being members of black or minority ethnic (BME) groups[5] are significantly more likely to be living in poverty. Even after controlling for the influence of all of the other variables, people from BME groups are estimated to be over four times more likely to be in poverty than are people who self-identify as white.

The type of household a person lives in also influences the chances that they are living in poverty on the PSE measure. In particular it appears that single people and lone parents are more likely to be living in poverty. However, when all of the other variables are controlled for, the strength of this association weakens

---

[4] In this variable the standard Government Office areas of England have been collapsed to form larger areas: the North includes the North East, the North West, Merseyside and Yorkshire and Humber; the Midlands includes both the East and the West Midlands; and the South includes the Eastern Region, the South East (outside of London) and the South West.

[5] Members of BME groups have had to be collapsed into one category due to the small number of cases for each particular black and minority ethnic group. Not only is this procedure inelegant in that it masks huge variation in the housing and other circumstances of different BME groups, it is also culturally and politically troublesome. In the end, pragmatic concern to at least begin to examine the ethnic basis of poverty and home-ownership has won out over an interest in dealing with the specificities of the issue. All inferences concerning BME groups that follow need to be contextualised with a wide range of sometimes quite profound caveats.

considerably. This strongly suggests that on the PSE measure it is not household type per se which influences the odds of poverty but factors that are associated with different types of household, in particular tenure, age and employment differences.

The data in Table 3 suggests that there are enduring differences in the experience of poverty between the sexes. On the PSE measure, women constitute 58% of all of those in poverty.

Finally, the association between poverty rates and current marital status initially appears significant – while just 19% of married people are in poverty on the PSE measure, almost 40% of divorced people are defined as such. However, when all of the other variables are controlled for the association becomes insignificant. Again, rather than it being marital status per se which impacts on the odds of living in poverty it is other factors associated with differences in marital status that are important.

The bottom household income quintile measure of poverty

Table 4 shows parallel data on the sociodemographic characteristics of those defined as being in poverty when the low income measure of poverty is used. On this measure the influence of housing tenure on the odds of poverty, although still significant, becomes less important than the number of workers in the household, the social class of the head of household, age and ethnicity. Not surprisingly the impact of differences in the number of people employed in a household has by far the greatest influence on the odds of being in poverty on the low income measure of poverty. Among those households with no one in work, 43% are defined as being in poverty (that is 72% of all of those in poverty).

The impact of social class on the odds of poverty remains important on this measure, as do differences in age and ethnicity. However, the relationship between age and the odds of poverty differs somewhat to that found using the PSE measure. On the low income measure, some 48% of those aged 75 and over are defined as living in poverty – the highest of all age groups. However, when all of the other variables have

been controlled for it is those aged 16 to 24 and 35 to 44 who are the most likely to be in poverty, and those aged between 45 and 74 who are the least likely.

The pattern of association between poverty and housing tenure is still significant and pronounced using the low income measure of poverty. Almost one half of those living in the social rented sector live in households with incomes in the bottom income quintile. In the PRS over one quarter of people live in such households. However, among outright owners the figure is 18% and among people buying their property with a mortgage the figure is just 10%. However, this still means that, among those defined as living in poverty on the low income measure, 48% (again, the modal category) are owner occupiers, 43% live in the social rented sector and, again, 9% live in the PRS. The strength of this association still holds when it is adjusted for the influence of the other variables. The impact of tenure on poverty on this measure is nowhere near as pronounced as on the PSE measure. Housing tenure still exerts an independent influence on the odds of living in poverty but other factors are far more important. After controlling for the other variables those living in social housing are still significantly more likely and outright owners are significantly less likely to live in poverty than are other people. Interestingly, on this measure, after the other variables are controlled for people buying a property with a mortgage are no more or no less likely to be living in poverty than are people living in the PRS.

The Bradshaw and Finch measure of poverty

The Bradshaw and Finch measure of poverty provides an indication of those who are in the most extreme of circumstances – in need on at least three and sometimes four different dimensions (see Table 5). For the population as whole just 8% of people are defined as being in this form of 'deep' poverty. However, among households with no workers the rate is almost one fifth. In terms of age, it is those between 25 and 44 who are the most likely to be found in this form of poverty; the ratio of females to males is 2:1. Among lone parents it is almost 30%, and for those living in the social rented sector it is one quarter.

Table 4: Bottom income quintile poverty measure sociodemographics

Variable	% in poverty	% of poor	Number	Adjusted odds
All	20	100	1,384	
*Tenure***				+++ [△LLR 20.2]
Owned outright	18	26	396	0.6**
Buying with a mortgage	10	22	645	0.8
Social housing	49	43	247	1.5**
Private rented sector	26	9	93	1.4
*Social class of head of household****				+++ [△LLR 35.6]
I	3	1	119	0.2***
II	12	17	373	0.6
IIIN	20	16	210	0.9
IIIM	20	27	362	1
IV	33	27	220	1.7
V	46	10	59	2.1*
Students	19	2	26	0.2
Army	68	1	[3]	3
*Number of workers in household****				+++ [△LLR 97.1]
0	43	72	468	1
1	14	17	345	0.2***
2	5	8	466	0.1***
3	4	1	90	0.1***
4	2	1	[15]	0.2***
*Age****				+++ [△LLR 31.2]
16-24	25	11	117	2.0*
25-34	15	14	257	1
35-44	19	16	237	2.1**
45-54	10	8	225	0.6*
55-64	14	12	228	0.6*
65-74	24	16	182	0.6*
75+	48	24	138	1.2
*Region***				ns
North	23	28	335	-
Midlands	20	17	232	-
South	18	29	434	-
London	18	10	150	-
Wales	17	7	106	-
Scotland	24	11	127	-
*Ethnicity****				+++ [△ LLR 21.1]
White	19	93	1,336	1.0
Black or minority ethnic group	42	7	48	4.6***
*Type of household****				ns
Single person	31	30	267	-
Couple with no dependent children	18	29	450	-
Couple with dependent children	13	25	536	-
Lone mother	35	14	108	-
Lone father	36	2	[14]	-
Gay couple	0	0	[9]	-
*Gender***				ns
Male	17	40	660	-
Female	23	60	724	-
*Current marital status****				ns
Single, never married	20	22	300	-
Married	16	45	801	-
Separated	33	4	36	-
Divorced	24	11	126	-
Widowed	41	18	121	-

Table 5: Bradshaw and Finch poverty measure sociodemographics

Variable	% in poverty	% of poor	Number	
All	8	100	1,215	Adjusted odds
*Tenure***				+++ [△LLR 20.2]
Owned outright	3	10	343	0.4*
Buying with a mortgage	4	22	566	1
Social housing	25	61	222	2.1**
Private rented sector	9	8	81	1.1
*Social class of head of household***				ns
I	0	0	100	–
II	4	16	327	–
IIIN	8	17	180	–
IIIM	7	25	321	–
IV	13	29	198	–
V	15	9	54	–
Students	15	3	[20]	–
Army	50	1	[2]	–
*Number of workers in household***				+++[△LLR 71.1]
0	19	83	410	1.0
1	4	12	308	0.2***
2	1	3	415	0.1***
3	3	2	71	0.1***
4	0	0	[12]	0.2***
*Age***				+++ [△ LLR 25.1]
16-24	8	8	86	0.9
25-34	10	26	243	2.8**
35-44	9	22	214	3.4***
45-54	7	14	199	1.2
55-64	7	15	203	1.0
65-74	5	9	160	0.4*
75+	6	7	109	0.4*
*Region***				ns
North	8	25	308	–
Midlands	6	13	212	–
South	7	27	381	–
London	7	10	128	–
Wales	13	12	83	–
Scotland	13	14	104	–
*Ethnicity***				ns
White	7	94	1,178	–
Black or minority ethnic group	16	7	37	–
*Type of household***				+ [△ LLR 35.6]
Single person	10	24	227	1.2
Couple with no dependent children	5	22	399	1.1
Couple with dependent children	4	19	467	0.9
Lone mother	28	31	103	3.9*
Lone father	30	4	[13]	7.9*
Gay couple	0	0	[7]	0.0
*Gender***				ns
Male	5	32	601	–
Female	10	68	614	–
*Current marital status***				ns
Single, never married	11	30	249	–
Married	4	29	713	–
Separated	24	9	34	–
Divorced	18	23	116	–
Widowed	9	10	116	–

Table 6: Summary of extent of poverty among home owners across the three different measures of poverty

	PSE measure		Bottom household income quintile measure		Bradshaw and Finch measure	
	% in poverty	% of poor	% in poverty	% of poor	% in poverty	% of poor
Outright owners	15	18	18	26	3	10
Buying with a mortgage	17	32	10	22	4	22
All home owners		50		48		32

This form of extreme poverty is relatively rare in the owner-occupied sector – just 3% of outright owners and just 4% of people buying a property with a mortgage are defined as such. However, because of the relative size of the owner-occupied sector, this still means that almost one third (32%) of people who are defined as being in poverty on this, the most circumscribed of the three measures of poverty considered in this report, are in the owner-occupied sector.

It is apparent from the above discussion that the manner in which poverty is operationalised influences the segments of the population defined as such. Nevertheless, the broad patterns of association are similar: poverty is associated with differences in tenure, class, employment status, age, ethnicity, gender, household structure, region and so on.

Our focus here, within this broader contextualisation of the social bases of poverty, is on differences in poverty across the housing tenures. We can conclude that differences in housing tenure exert an independent influence on the odds that someone is in poverty, but that the efficacy of this influence varies with different operationalisations of poverty. Using the PSE measure, differences in housing tenure appear as one of the most important influences on the odds of poverty, whereas on the other two, more restricted measures of poverty, the influence of differences in housing tenure is not as strong.

We can also note that, as the definition of poverty becomes more and more restricted, the proportion of those in poverty who are home owners – the focus of our concern here – decreases. This is shown in summary form in Table 6. On the broadest definition of poverty examined here (the PSE measure) home owners

do indeed form half of the poor. However, on the strictest definition home owners form only one third of the poor. If one just considers those buying property with a mortgage we can see that on the broadest definition they form almost one third of those in poverty, while on the other two, more restricted, measures they still form over one fifth (22% in both cases) of the poor.

In the next chapter of the report we examine some of the characteristics of home owners who are defined as being in poverty on each of the three measures.

The characteristics of home owners who are in poverty

In this chapter we summarise some of the socioeconomic characteristics of home owners – both mortgagors and outright owners – who are defined as living in poverty on each of the three measures of poverty discussed previously.

The PSE measure of poverty

Table 7 shows the overall poverty rates, using the PSE measure, for outright owners (15%) and mortgagors (17%) and then examines how these rates vary across a range of different sociodemographic characteristics. In this and subsequent tables, cell counts sometimes fall to very small numbers and rates calculated on the basis of numbers less than 20 are, for the most part, ignored in the discussion. Logistic regression models have also been calculated and the most significant predictors of poverty are also shown. We begin with mortgagors and then discuss outright owners.

Among *mortgagors*, those most likely to be in poverty on the PSE measure are:

- those living in households with no workers: a full one third of mortgagors with no household members currently in work are living in poverty, while those with two household members currently in employment are the least likely to live in poverty – just 13%;
- lone parent households;
- young mortgagors[6] aged between 25 and 34, some 27% of whom are living in poverty on this measure;
- households headed by someone from a manual social class background; for instance just 2% of households headed by someone

from social class I are defined as living in poverty, compared to a full one third of those headed by someone in social class IV;
- people who self-identify as members of a BME group: over one half of BME group mortgagors are in poverty;
- households residing in the Midlands or, in particular, Wales;
- people who have experienced divorce or separation.

Among *outright owners* the correlates of poverty are similar although mediated by the rather different age profile of the group. Outright owners:

- still with a substantial foothold in the labour market are *less likely* than other outright owning households to be in poverty – just 9% of households with two workers are in poverty compared to the 16% of those households with no workers;
- based on a single person (with or without children) household are more likely to be in poverty than other household types;
- who are younger than the average are more likely to be in poverty (cf Sullivan and Murphy, 1987);
- headed by someone from a manual social class background are more likely to be in poverty;

---

6   This variable measures the characteristics of the respondent rather than the household in which they live, which means that some will be living in the parental home (especially those aged 16 to 24) and will not have direct responsibility for mortgage payments. However, the majority of those aged 25 to 34 are living independently (Rugg and Burrows, 1999).

Table 7: Poverty rates among home owners using the PSE measure

Variable	Mortgagors in poverty (%)	n	Adjusted odds	Outright owners in poverty (%)	n	Adjusted odds
All	17	724		15	447	
Number of workers in household			+++[△ LLR 23.5]			ns
0	33	60	1.0	16	250	
1	18	113	0.3***	18	96	
2	13	380	0.1***	9	68	
3	27	76	0.2***	17	30	
4	7	14	0.2	0	[4]	
Type of household			++[△ LLR 18.4]			ns
Single person	13	78	0.3**	23	105	
Couple with no dependent children	10	187	0.3**	12	217	
Couple with dependent children	19	409	0.7	15	107	
Lone mother	35	37	1.1	27	[15]	
Lone father	57	[7]	2.7	0	[3]	
Gay couple	43	[7]	5.6	0	[2]	
Age			+++[△ LLR 31.9]			ns
16-24	14	72	2.6	25	[16]	
25-34	27	188	4.3***	0	[5]	
35-44	12	190	0.8	32	[19]	
45-54	18	158	1.9	10	49	
55-64	12	92	0.9	14	128	
65-74	14	21	0.3	15	135	
75+	0	[4]	0.2	15	94	
Social class of head of household			+++[△ LLR 35.3]			ns
I	2	96	0.1***	4	28	
II	11	204	0.5*	10	141	
IIIN	18	119	1.1	15	75	
IIIM	23	211	1.4	20	106	
IV	33	67	3.0**	26	77	
V	21	[14]	1.8	14	[14]	
Students	43	[14]	2.5	0	[1]	
Army	0	0	-	0	[1]	
Ethnicity			+++[△ LLR 20.9]			+[△ LLR 6.5]
White	15	684	1.0	15	439	1.0
Black or minority ethnic group	56	33	6.7***	50	[8]	6.5*
Region			ns			ns
North	13	151		13	134	
Midlands	23	160		28	61	
South	14	203		13	168	
London	16	83		15	27	
Wales	29	55		19	32	
Scotland	14	72		8	26	
Gender			ns			ns
Male	15	351		13	224	
Female	9	374		18	223	
Current marital status			+[△ LLR 12.4]			+[△ LLR 6.0]
Single, never married	13	166	0.4*	16	4	0.6
Married	17	468	1.5	13	299	0.6*
Separated	32	[16]	1.0	33	[6]	1.7
Divorced	30	64	2.0	33	27	2.0
Widowed	8	[12]	0.7	17	71	0.9

- from BME groups are more likely to be in poverty (although note that the base number is very low);
- who are female are more likely to be in poverty (18% compared to 13% of males);
- who are divorced or separated are more likely to be in poverty.

The bottom household income quintile measure of poverty

Table 8 shows the overall poverty rates, using the bottom household income quintile measure, for outright owners (18%) and mortgagors (10%), and then examines how these rates vary across a range of different sociodemographic characteristics.

Among *mortgagors*, those most likely to be in poverty on the bottom quintile measure are:

- those living in households with no workers: 45% of mortgagors with no household members currently in work are living in poverty, while those with two household members currently in employment are the least likely to be in poverty – just 3%;
- lone parent households: about one quarter are in poverty;
- young(er) mortgagors, although the age-related profile of poverty is rather different to that found using the PSE measure;
- households headed by someone from a manual social class background;
- people who self-identify as members of a BME group;
- households residing in the North;
- people who have experienced divorce or separation.

Among *outright owners*:

- those with no workers in the household are the most likely to be in poverty – almost 30%;
- households based on a single person or couples with no dependant children are more likely to be in poverty than other household types (although this association is clearly related to age);
- those who are older are more likely to be in poverty – almost 40% of outright owners aged 75 and over are in poverty on this measure;

- households headed by someone from a manual social class background are more likely to be in poverty;
- females are more likely to be in poverty (23% compared to 14% of males), but, again, this is likely to be age related;
- those who are widowed are more likely to be in poverty – over one third of outright owners who are widowed are living in poverty on this measure.

The Bradshaw and Finch measure of poverty

Table 9 shows the overall poverty rates, using the Bradshaw and Finch measure, for outright owners (3%) and mortgagors (4%), and then examines how these rates vary across a range of different sociodemographic characteristics.

Among *mortgagors*, those most likely to be in poverty are:

- those living in households with no workers;
- lone parent households;
- young(er) mortgagor households – this becomes especially apparent when the odds of poverty are adjusted;
- households headed by someone from a manual social class background;
- households residing in Wales;
- people who have experienced divorce or separation.

Among *outright owners*:

- those with no workers in the household are the most likely to be in poverty;
- those who are older are marginally more likely to be in poverty;
- households headed by someone from a manual social class background are more likely to be in poverty;
- households living in Wales are most likely to be living poverty;
- females are twice as likely as men to be living poverty, but, again, this is likely to be age related;
- those who are divorced are the most likely to be living in poverty.

Table 8: Poverty rates among home owners using the bottom income quintile measure

Variable	Mortgagors in poverty (%)	n	Adjusted odds	Outright owners in poverty (%)	n	Adjusted odds
All	10	645		18	396	
Number of workers in household			+++[△ LLR 71.9]			+++[△ LLR 43.4]
0	45	51	1.0	29	222	1.0
1	11	178	0.1***	3	88	0.1**
2	3	356	0.1***	8	52	0.2**
3	6	48	0.1***	3	30	0.1*
4	36	[11]	0.1*	0	[4]	–
Type of household			ns			ns
Single person	6	67		28	96	
Couple with no dependent children	8	171		20	190	
Couple with dependent children	9	356		7	93	
Lone mother	22	36		8	[12]	
Lone father	29	[7]		0	[3]	
Gay couple	0	[7]		0	[2]	
Age			+++[△ LLR 25.5]			ns
16-24	18	72	4.6***	20	[10]	
25-34	2	165	0.5	0	[5]	
35-44	13	172	3.4**	13	[16]	
45-54	6	135	0.7	5	44	
55-64	10	79	0.6	8	113	
65-74	16	19	0.3	20	124	
75+	63	[3]	1.0	38	84	
Social class of head of household			+[△ LLR 16.4]			ns
I	1	85	0.1*	4	23	
II	8	186	0.7	12	126	
IIIN	10	107	0.8	21	66	
IIIM	11	177	1.4	24	98	
IV	14	66	2.0	23	65	
V	30	[10]	5.1	21	[14]	
Students	18	[11]	0.9	0	[1]	
Army	0	0	–	0	[1]	
Ethnicity			+[△ LLR 4.1]			ns
White	9	616	1.0	18	395	
Black or minority ethnic group	25	28	3.3*	100	[1]	
Region			ns			ns
North	13	145		18	117	
Midlands	9	128		24	50	
South	9	180		16	147	
London	4	81		24	25	
Wales	10	49		13	32	
Scotland	10	63		20	25	
Gender	ns	ns				
Male	10	305		14	202	
Female	10	339		23	194	
Current marital status			ns			ns
Single, never married	10	154		16	38	
Married	9	409		15	267	
Separated	13	[15]		20	[5]	
Divorced	11	55		8	24	
Widowed	9	[11]		35	63	

Table 9: Poverty rates among home owners using the Bradshaw and Finch Measure

Variable	Mortgagors in poverty (%)	n	Adjusted odds	Outright owners in poverty (%)	n	Adjusted odds
All	4	566		3	343	
Number of workers in household			+++[△ LLR 77.8]			ns
0	31	48	1.0	4	188	
1	2	162	0.1***	1	77	
2	0	315	0.1***	2	6	
3		32	0.1**		29	
4	0	[8]	–	0	[4]	
Type of household			ns			ns
Single person	3	61		4	78	
Couple with no dependent children	2	58		3	163	
Couple with dependent children	2	300		2	85	
Lone mother	17	35		8	[12]	
Lone father	33	[6]		0	[3]	
Gay couple	0	[5]		0	[2]	
Age			+[△ LLR 18.2]			ns
16-24	2	48	2.9	0	[9]	
25-34	2	152	4.8	0	[5]	
35-44	5	155	10.2**	0	[11]	
45-54	3	123	0.7	3	38	
55-64	5	67	0.2*	3	104	
65-74	6	[17]	0.2	4	110	
75+	0	[2]	0.2	2	66	
Social class of head of household			ns			ns
I	0	74		0	[17]	
II	3	165		2	106	
IIIN	2	88		2	57	
IIIM	5	155		3	89	
IV	5	62		3	59	
V	0	[1]		8	[13]	
Students	18	[11]		0	0	
Army	0	0		0	0	
Ethnicity			ns			ns
White	4	546		3	342	
Black or minority ethnic group	5	20		0	[1]	
Region			ns			ns
North	5	133		4	108	
Midlands	1	120		2	44	
South	4	159		2	129	
London	0	64		4	23	
Wales	8	38		5	22	
Scotland	6	52		0	18	
Gender			ns			ns
Male	3	278		2	184	
Female	4	288		4	159	
Current marital status			ns			ns
Single, never married	3	122		3	31	
Married	2	367		2	236	
Separated	13	[15]		0	[4]	
Divorced	12	52		10	20	
Widowed	0	[11]		4	53	

Concluding comment

In this chapter we have shown how the characteristics of home owners who are living in poverty varies in relation to the measurement of poverty used. In the next chapter we examine how the characteristics of those who are defined as living in poverty varies in relation to housing tenure.

6

Poverty profiles: differences between poor home owners and the poor living in other tenures

Another way of examining the characteristics of home owners living in poverty is to compare their characteristics with people living in other housing tenures who are also defined as being poor. The number of cases available for analysis of this sort is quite small and therefore it is necessary to collapse the housing tenure variable down into just two categories: home owners (outright owners and mortgagors together) and renters (those in the social rented sector and the PRS together).

The PSE measure of poverty

Table 10 examines the different sociodemographic characteristics of those defined as living in poverty using the PSE measure split by housing tenure. The number of cases available for analysis is small, but some useful descriptions of the differences between the poor in the two tenures is possible, as is some simple multivariate analysis. As we have seen above (Table 6, p 18), on the PSE measure, the poor are almost exactly equally split between the two main tenures: in our data 193 are home owners and 192 are renters. Table 10 suggests that:

- Poor home owners are more likely to live in households in which people are in employment. Among the poor living in home ownership just under one third (32%) live in households in which no one works, whereas among the poor living in the rented sector the figure is over two thirds (68%).
- The age profile of the poor also differs somewhat across the tenures: the poor living in the rented sector tend to be younger than poor home owners.

- There are clear social class differences with a far higher proportion of poor home owners coming from either non-manual (37%) or skilled manual backgrounds (37%), whereas the majority (71%) of poor renters are from manual class backgrounds.
- There also exist some regional differences; in the North, the South, London and Scotland similar or higher proportions of the poor live in the rented sector than are home owners, whereas in the Midlands and Wales higher proportions of the poor are home owners than live in the rented sector.
- Poor home owners are more likely to be members of a BME group than are poor renters: 14% of poor home owners are from a BME group compared to just 8% of poor renters.
- Poor renters are more likely to live as single people (30% compared to 18%) or to be lone parents (25% compared to 11%) than are poor home owners; almost one half (48%) of poor home owners are couples with dependent children compared to just over one quarter (26%) of renters.
- Poor home owners are more likely to be married than poor renters (60% compared to 28%); poor renters are more likely to be single (40% compared to 15%).

The adjusted odds show that the best predictors that someone who is poor is a home owner are (in order of importance):

- whether or not someone in the household is working;
- the social class of the head of household;
- age;
- current marital status;
- ethnicity.

Table 10: Tenure differences in the sociodemographic characteristics of the poor using the PSE measure

Variable	Home owners (%)	Renters (%)	Adjusted odds that PSE poor will be home owners
Number of workers in household			+++[△LLR 53.2]
0	32	68	1.0
1	27	23	5.3***
2	28	8	20.0***
3+	14	2	25.0
Age			+++[△LLR 26.2]
16-24	7	15	0.8
25-34	26	28	0.2***
35-44	15	13	0.6
45-54	17	15	0.6
55-64	15	12	1.6
65-74	12	8	4.7***
75+	8	9	2.0
Social class of head of household			+++[△LLR 36.1]
I	2	1	2.9
II	18	9	5.3*
IIIN	17	14	3.3
IIIM	37	26	1.8
IV	21	32	0.7
V	3	13	0.3
Other	3	5	0.1
Region			ns
North	20	24	
Midlands	28	18	
South	26	28	
London	9	10	
Wales	12	10	
Scotland	6	9	
Ethnicity			++[△LLR 7.6]
White	86	92	1.0
Black or minority ethnic group	14	8	4.2**
Type of household			ns
Single person	18	30	
Couple with no dependent children	22	19	
Couple with dependent children	48	26	
Lone parent	11	25	
Gender			ns
Male	43	42	
Female	57	58	
Current marital status			++[△LLR 16.2]
Single, never married	15	40	0.4**
Married	60	28	2.5*
Separated	4	6	1.1
Divorced	15	14	1.7
Widowed	7	13	0.6
Base n	*193*	*192*	

The bottom household income quintile measure of poverty

Table 11 examines the different sociodemographic characteristics of those defined as living in poverty using the bottom household income quintile measure, split by housing tenure. As we have seen in Table 6 (p 18), on this measure, the poor are again roughly equally split between the two main tenures – in our data 133 are home owners and 144 are renters. The number of cases means that multivariate analysis is not possible. On this measure:

- Although poor home owners are more likely to live in households in which people are in employment, the differences are not as great (65% compared to 78%) as when using the PSE measure.
- The age profile of the poor again differs somewhat across the tenures.
- On this measure, the regional differences are less stark with broadly similar proportions of the poor living in each tenure. The one exception might be Scotland, where a higher proportion lives in the rented sector.
- On this measure, poor home owners are less likely to be members of a BME group than are poor renters – 5% of poor home owners are from a BME group compared to 9% of poor renters.
- Poor renters are, again, more likely to live as single people or to be lone parents than are poor home owners.
- Poor home owners are, again, more likely to be married than poor renters. Poor renters are more likely to be single and, on this measure, poor renters are more likely to be divorced or separated.

Table 11: Tenure differences in the sociodemographic characteristics of the poor using the bottom income quintile measure

Variable	Home owners (%)	Renters (%)
Number of workers in household		
0	65	78
1	18	17
2	11	6
3+	6	0
Age		
16-24	11	10
25-34	3	24
35-44	19	14
45-54	8	9
55-64	14	10
65-74	22	11
75+	25	22
Social class of head of household		
I	2	1
II	22	12
IIIN	19	12
IIIM	32	23
IV	19	34
V	5	15
Other	2	3
*Region***		
North	31	26
Midlands	17	16
South	31	26
London	12	13
Wales	7	6
Scotland	8	13
*Ethnicity****		
White	95	91
Black or minority ethnic group	5	9
*Type of household****		
Single person	24	36
Couple with no dependent children	39	20
Couple with dependent children	29	22
Lone parent	8	22
*Gender***		
Male	43	38
Female	57	62
*Current marital status****		
Single, never married	16	28
Married	59	33
Separated	2	6
Divorced	6	15
Widowed	17	18
Base n	*133*	*144*

The Bradshaw and Finch measure of poverty

Table 12 examines the different sociodemographic characteristics of those defined as living in poverty using the Bradshaw and Finch measure, split by housing tenure. As we have seen in Table 6 (p 18), on this measure, the number of cases available for analysis falls to very low numbers – just 30 cases for home owners and 64 cases for renters. With such low cell counts it is impossible to make any clear inferences, although the broad patterns of association are clear enough and are, for the most part, similar to those found in Tables 10 and 11. The Table is included here for the sake of analytic completeness.

Table 12: Tenure differences in the sociodemographic characteristics of the poor using the Bradshaw and Finch measure

Variable	Home owners (%)	Renters (%)
Number of workers in household		
0	73	86
1	13	13
2	7	2
3+	7	0
Age		
16-24	3	10
25-34	10	34
35-44	24	19
45-54	17	13
55-64	21	13
65-74	17	5
75+	7	7
Social class of head of household		
I	0	0
II	24	12
IIIN	14	18
IIIM	35	35
IV	17	12
V	3	2
Other	7	2
Region		
North	37	22
Midlands	8	16
South	32	25
London	4	13
Wales	14	11
Scotland	11	14
Ethnicity		
White	97	92
Black or minority ethnic group	3	8
Type of household		
Single person	17	27
Couple with no dependent children	21	22
Couple with dependent children	31	16
Lone parent	31	36
Gender		
Male	40	29
Female	60	71
Current marital status		
Single, never married	14	38
Married	41	23
Separated	10	9
Divorced	28	20
Widowed	7	9
Base n	*30*	*64*

7

Differences in the nature of poverty between the tenures

We have now explored the differences in the *extent* of poverty across the housing tenures and have examined some of the major sociodemographic *differences* between the poor living in the different tenures. We now briefly turn to an examination of some differences in the *nature* of the poverty experienced in the tenures.

In all of the three measures we have used we have taken a distinct cut-off point to define whether or not someone is, or is not, living in poverty. However, an examination of the extent of the poverty across the tenures would strongly suggest that both the intensity and the form of the poverty being experienced by people living in different housing tenures may well be far more complex than a simple 'poverty line' allows us to indicate. We can explore some of this diversity in the nature of poverty by examining how both the ownership of socially perceived necessities and incomes vary for those in poverty across the tenures. This is shown in Table 13.

On all three measures of poverty, on average, poor owner occupiers possess a greater number of socially perceived necessities than do poor renters, although on the Bradshaw and Finch

measure the difference is not statistically significant. For example, on the PSE measure of poverty poor home owners lack an average of 5.8 necessities, while poor renters lack 6.6 necessities (p<0.05).

On two of the measures of poverty poor home owners possess significantly higher average household incomes than do poor renters. For example, on the PSE measure, poor home owners have an average weekly income of £241 compared to poor renters who have just £197 (p<0.001). However, on the Bradshaw and Finch measure there are no significant differences in average incomes.

We thus conclude that, when using the maximalist and intermediate measures of poverty, the poor in the owner-occupied sector are, on average, less deprived than the poor living in the rented tenures – all are poor but the very poorest are not home owners. However, when one uses the minimalist definition of poverty, such tenure differences all but disappear: among the very poorest, tenure differences make no or little difference to the intensity of the experience

Table 13: Differences in the number of socially perceived necessities lacking and average incomes by tenure across the three measures of poverty

	Average number of socially perceived necessities lacking			Average equivalised weekly net household incomes		
	PSE	Bottom quintile	Bradshaw and Finch	PSE	Bottom quintile	Bradshaw and Finch
Owner occupiers	5.8*	2.6***	7.5	£241***	£122*	£133
Renters	6.6	4.8	8.5	£197	£111	£150

In the next chapter we begin to examine systematically a range of other differences between the poor living in the owner-occupied sector compared to the poor living in the other tenures. However, for the rest of the report we will only use the PSE measure of poverty. The reasons for this are essentially pragmatic – in order to be able to decipher any statistically significant differences in poverty outcomes across the tenures we need a measure that will maximise the number of cases available for analysis. We begin by analysing differences in housing circumstances (other than tenure of course); we then consider a range of different measures of health and well-being. We conclude the chapter by examining a range of different measures of the experience of social exclusion.

8

Poverty outcomes: (how) does tenure make a difference?

There is now a large social scientific literature which examines both the positive (for example, Ellaway and MacIntyre, 1998) and negative (for example, Nettleton and Burrows, 2000; Smith et al, 2002) aspects of owner occupation in relation to a range of different health and social outcomes. However, hitherto there have been few systematic attempts to examine how the experience of poverty is mediated by differences in housing tenure. Here we begin this task by examining how the poor living in different housing tenures report a range of different outcomes relating to housing, health and various aspects of social exclusion. We begin by describing the data in very simple bivariate terms. We then move on to examine a small number of different outcomes within a multivariate framework.

Housing

Table 14 shows how the poor – on the PSE measure – experience their current accommodation across the two main tenures.

People who are defined as poor who rent are significantly more likely than are poor home owners to live in flats (as opposed to houses). They are also significantly more likely to be very dissatisfied with the neighbourhoods within which they reside. However, when it comes to evaluations of the quality of accommodation there are very few differences between the two tenure groups. Home owners are significantly more likely to report leaky roofs, but on other measures of problems with the built fabric no significant differences exist.

Table 14: Comparison of quality of accommodation and neighbourhood of the poor across tenure (%)

	Home owners	Renters
Flats***	9	36
Very dissatisfied with neighbourhood***	4	10
1 Shortage of space	36	31
2 Too dark, not enough light	5	7
3 Lack of adequate heating facilities	16	13
4 Leaky roof**	13	4
5 Damp walls or floors	18	16
6 Rot in window frames or floors	21	17
7 Mould	11	10
8 No place to sit outside, eg garden or terrace	8	14
9 Other problem	6	8
Average number of problems (0-9)	1.2	1.3
No problems with accommodation	34	37
State of repair poor	15	17
n	193	192

Health and well-being

Table 15 shows differences in various measures of health and well-being among the poor living in different housing tenures. The simple bivariate results suggest that significant differences exist between the proportions that report that their general health is not good and/or that they have a long-standing illness or disability of some sort. Poor renters also report significantly higher rates of smoking than do home owners – although both are high (55%

Table 15: Comparison of health and well-being of the poor across tenure (%)

	Home owners	Renters
General health not good*	18	29
Long-standing illness or disability***	35	54
Average number of illnesses	1.8	1.9
Seen GP in last two weeks?	18	24
Outpatient in last three months?	15	21
Inpatient in last 12 months?	10	14
Visit to accident and emergency in last 12 months?	18	25
Smoke now?*	55	68
Average number smoked per day	14	16.2
Average number of units of alcohol per week	9.4	12.8
GHQ12[a]	26.4	25.3

Note: [a] A common measure of psychiatric morbidity (significant at $p=0.09$)[7].

Table 16: Comparison of different experiences of social exclusion among the poor across tenure (%)

	Home owners	Renters
Labour market excluded***	11	44
Ever disconnected from utilities?	14	20
Ever used utilities less than needed?***	24	38
Two or more public/private services lacking	36	40
Do not see/speak to family/ friends daily*	15	8
Lacks social support in four or more areas	17	22
Feel unsafe out at night?	34	41
Feel unsafe alone at home?	18	16
Voted?*	73	60
Excluded in any way?	92	90
Disengaged but voted?	37	44
Excluded in all ways***	20	39
Labour market excluded + excluded in any other way***	21	58

compared to 68%). However, on all of the other measures no significant differences are apparent.

The disproportionate numbers of people in the rented sector (especially the social rented sector) is, of course, as much a function of 'health selection' processes of various sorts (for example, medical priority for rehousing, the acceptance of someone as homeless because of vulnerabilities of different types and so on), as it is of the material and psychological impact of housing and neighbourhood circumstances on health per se (Smith et al, 2002). However, as we have seen, we are also dealing with two rather different populations here (in terms of age, gender, employment status and so on) and so we need to build in various statistical controls to deal with these population differences if we want to evaluate the impact of differences in housing on

these health measures. We attempt this in the next section of the report.

Social exclusion

Table 16 examines different measures of social exclusion as developed by the PSE survey team (Gordon et al, 2000, Chapter 5). They distinguish between four different dimensions of social exclusion: poverty (which we have been discussing), labour market exclusion, service exclusion and exclusion from social relations. Significantly:

- more poor renters than poor home owners are excluded from the labour market;
- more poor renters than poor home owners have had to cut back on the use of basic utilities (power, water and so on);
- more poor home owners than poor renters lack ongoing social support from family and friends;
- more poor renters than poor home owners fail to vote;
- more poor renters than poor home owners are excluded on all four dimensions.

---

[7] The General Health Questionnaire (GHQ12) is used to detect the presence of non-psychotic psychiatric morbidity in community settings and is a widely employed measure of well-being. The questionnaire comprises 12 questions, asking informants about their general level of happiness, experience of depressive and anxiety symptoms, and sleep disturbance over the last four weeks. Interpretation of the answers is based on a four-point response scale (0-3) generating possible scores between 0 (best) and 36 (worst).

Multivariate analysis of tenure differences in poverty outcomes

These bivariate differences in poverty outcomes may simply be a function of the different socioeconomic characteristics of the poor living in the two tenure groups – differences detailed for the PSE measure in Table 10. In the analysis that follows we select a number of key variables from Tables 14, 15 and 16 and subject them to a logistic regression analysis in order to examine if differences in poverty outcomes between home owners and renters endure once these socioeconomic differences have been controlled for. In order to do this we need to construct a set of dichotomous measures from those already considered. The measures we consider are as follows:

- very dissatisfied with neighbourhood
- more than one problem with accommodation
- accommodation in poor state of repair
- general health not good
- smoke now
- worst 20% of GHQ12 scores among the poor
- lacks social support in four or more areas[8]
- did not vote
- excluded in all ways.

For each of these measures we have calculated the adjusted odds that poor renters compared to home owners possess the attribute in question, after controlling for the influence of the three major socioeconomic differences between the populations in the two tenure groups (see Table 10): the number of workers in the household, age, and the social class of the head of household. If the adjusted odds ratio is 1.0 there exist no differences between the odds that a person possesses the attribute in question across the tenures once the influence of these three variables has been adjusted for. If the figure is greater than 1.0 this indicates that renters are more likely to possess the attribute; if the figure is less than 1.0 this indicates that home owners

---

Table 17: Adjusted odds of a range of poverty outcomes among PSE poor renters compared to PSE poor home owners: odds adjusted for number of workers in the household, age and the social class of the head of household

	Adjusted odds
Very dissatisfied with neighbourhood	1.3
More than one problem with accommodation	0.8
Accommodation in poor state of repair	0.8
General health not good	1.2
Smoke now	1.8*
Worse 20% of GHQ12 scores	0.8
Lacks social support in four or more areas	1.6
Did not vote	1.5
Excluded in all ways	1.9*

* Significant at $p<0.05$.

are more likely to possess the attribute. If the differences are statistically significant this is also indicated.

The results of this multivariate exercise (see Table 17) show that, when other variables are controlled for, the poverty outcomes for the poor in the two tenures shows a clear patterning. First, there are few, if any significant differences in housing-related outcomes. Poor renters are more likely to be very dissatisfied with their neighbourhoods but poor home owners are more likely to report a problem with their accommodation. None of these differences are statistically significant. Second, in relation to poverty-related health outcomes, poor renters are significantly more likely to smoke than are poor home owners ($p<0.05$) and are also more likely to report that their general health is not good. However, poor home owners are more likely to report poor mental health than are poor renters (using the GHQ12 measure of psychiatric morbidity), although the difference is not significant. Third, poor renters are more likely to be socially excluded than are poor home owners; they are more likely to lack adequate social support, are more likely not to vote and are more likely to experience social exclusion on all of the dimensions considered.

---

[8] This measure is based on the identification of seven situations in which social support might be needed (eg advice; help with a heavy household job; someone to talk to if depressed; and so on). Those saying they would lack social support in four or more such situations are coded as 1, those who say they would have support in four or more such situations are coded 0.

These results are suggestive rather than definitive, of course, but they do point towards the hypothesis that the outcomes of poverty are at least mediated by differences in housing tenure. For renters, the outcomes of poverty primarily relate to unhealthy neighbourhoods, poor physical health, problematic health behaviours and profound processes of social and political exclusion. For poor home owners on the other hand, poverty outcomes primarily relate to problematic physical accommodation and poor mental health.

9

Concluding comments

This report has examined the extent and nature of poverty among home owners in Britain. We have concluded that the nature of poverty in general, and the nature of poverty among home owners in particular, is significantly affected by the way in which poverty is conceptualised and measured. That said, whatever definition of poverty one utilises, the proportion of the poor who are home owners is very much higher than one might have surmised from an acquaintance with the great bulk of previous research on poverty and housing policy. The report concludes that we can be confident in following Burrows and Wilcox (2000) in claiming that home owners constitute about half the poor in Britain. However, although home owners form about half the poor, the characteristics of poor home owners and poor renters differ markedly. The report has detailed many of these differences. The outcomes of poverty also appear to differ between the tenures, although the exact specification of these important differences will require more detailed work than is possible using the PSE Survey.

What are the implications of this conclusion? It suggests very clearly that we need to rethink dominant perceptions about poverty and housing tenure. We need to recognise that with the growth in home ownership it is now much less helpful than it was in the past to think of poverty in terms of renters and owners. This carries with it the need to be watchful that area-based policies to address poverty do not, inadvertently, exclude areas of poor home ownership.

The conclusion that home owners constitute half the poor also means that we need to rethink the tenure divide in state assistance with housing costs. Some of the inequities in the current provision for assistance with housing costs were

set out in the Preface to this report. They do not need to be repeated in detail here, but all remain pertinent and the case for a tenure-neutral housing allowance is a case based on both equity and the delivery of housing policy. The arguments raised against acting to assist poor home owners also need to be challenged. Here, the emphasis is typically placed on home owners' access to a capital asset, but this has to be placed in the context that, among low-income home owners, the asset is often modest and in any case not available to them during the lifetime of their occupancy. As such, it does not afford households a means to improve their standard of living or release resources to cover housing costs when faced with disruptions to income.

As has been noted elsewhere,

> whatever policy perspective is adopted there is [still] no justification for the current crude discrimination against low-income home owners in UK housing and social security policy.... The evidence on the relative costs of supporting low-income households in home-ownership, rather than renting, adds to the case for a fundamental review of current policy. If housing policies are, as suggested [in current policy documents and legislative proposals] to promote consumer choice, a more tenure neutral system of housing support for low-income households is required. (Burrows et al, 2000, pp 19-20).

Equally, it is not just objectives to deliver choice and sustainable home ownership that require more support for low-income home owners; policies to alleviate poverty also require the same housing allowances.

References

Bradshaw, J.R. (1972) 'The taxonomy of social need', in G. McLachlan (ed) *Problems and progress in medical care*, Oxford: Oxford University Press.

Bradshaw, J.R. (1994) 'The conceptualisation and measurement of need: a social policy perspective', in J. Popay and G. Williams (eds) *Researching the people's health*, London: Routledge.

Bradshaw, J.R. and Finch, N. (2001) 'Core poverty', Paper presented at a seminar at the *Centre for the Analysis of Social Exclusion, London School of Economics*, 7 March 2001. Available to download at www-users.york.ac.uk/~jrb1.

Burrows, R. and Rhodes, D. (2000) 'The geography of misery: area disadvantage and patterns of neighbourhood dissatisfaction in England', in J.R. Bradshaw and R. Sainsbury (eds) *Researching poverty*, Aldershot: Ashgate.

Burrows, R. and Wilcox, S. (2000) *Half the poor: Home owners with low incomes*, London: Council of Mortgage Lenders.

Burrows, R., Ford, J. and Wilcox, S. (2000) 'Half the poor? Policy responses to low income home ownership', in S. Wilcox (ed) *Housing finance review 2000/2001*, Coventry/London/York: Chartered Institute of Housing/Council of Mortgage Lenders/Joseph Rowntree Foundation.

Carter, J. (ed) (1998) *Postmodernity and the fragmentation of welfare*, London: Routledge.

Ellaway, A. and MacIntyre, S. (1998) 'Does housing tenure predict health in the UK because it exposes people to different levels of housing-related hazards in the home or its surroundings?', *Health and Place*, vol 4, no 2, pp 141-50.

Etzioni, A. (1998) 'Voluntary simplicity: characterization, select psychological implications and societal consequences', *Journal of Economic Psychology*, no 19, pp 619-43.

Ford, J., Burrows, R. and Nettleton, S. (2001) *Home ownership in a risk society: A social analysis of mortgage arrears and possession*, Bristol: The Policy Press.

Forrest, R. and Murie, A. (1990) *Residualisation and council housing*, SAUS Working Paper No 91, Bristol: SAUS Publications.

Gordon, D., Adelman, L., Ashworth, K., Bradshaw, J., Levitas, R., Middleton, S., Pantazis, C., Patsios, D., Payne, S., Townsend, P. and Williams, J. (2000) *Poverty and social exclusion in Britain*, York: Joseph Rowntree Foundation.

Hamnett, C. (1999) *Winners and losers: Home ownership in modern Britain*, London: UCL Press.

Lee, P and Murie, A. (1997) *Poverty, housing tenure and social exclusion*, Bristol/York: The Policy Press/Joseph Rowntree Foundation.

Nettleton, S. and Burrows, R. (2000) 'When a capital investment becomes an emotional loss: the health consequences of the experience of mortgage possession', *Housing Studies*, vol 15, no 3, pp 463-79.

Nettleton, S. and Burrows, R. (2001) 'Families coping with the experience of mortgage repossession in the "new landscape of precariousness"', *Community, Work and Family*, vol 4, no 3, pp 253-72.

Petersen, A., Barns, I., Dudley, J. and Harris, P. (1999) *Poststructuralism, citizenship and social policy*, London: Routledge.

Rugg, J. and Burrows, R. (1999) 'Setting the context: young people and housing', in J. Rugg (ed) *Young people, housing and social policy*, London: Routledge.

Sayer, A. (1984) *Method in social science: A realist approach*, London: Hutchinson.

Smith, S., Easterlow, D., Munro, M. and Turner, K. (2002) 'Housing as health capital: how health trajectories and housing paths are linked', *Journal of Social Issues* (in press).

Sullivan, O. and Murphy, M. (1987) 'Young outright owner occupiers in Britain', *Housing Studies*, vol 2, no 3, pp 177-91.

Wilcox, S. (2001) *Housing finance review 2001/2002*, Coventry/London/York: Chartered Institute of Housing/Council of Mortgage Lenders/Joseph Rowntree Foundation.

Also available from The Policy Press
Published in association with the Joseph Rowntree Foundation

Social market or safety net?
British social rented housing in a European context

Mark Stephens, Nicky Burns and Lisa MacKay
Social rented housing in Britain is undergoing radical reform – often inspired by European experiences. This timely report provides a comparative analysis of the social rented sector in seven European countries. Combined with analysis of labour market and social security systems, it challenges the assumptions behind the British reform agenda.

Paperback £12.95 ISBN 1 86134 387 6

Growing together or growing apart?
Geographic patterns of change of Income Support and income-based Jobseeker's Allowance claimants in England between 1995 and 2000

Martin Evans, Michael Noble, Gemma Wright, George Smith, Myfanwy Lloyd and Chris Dibben
Between 1995 and 2000 there has been a period of strong economic growth and a drop in claimant-based unemployment rates, but has everyone in every area of England benefited equally? Drawing on data from the Department of Work and Pensions about claimants of Income Support and Jobseeker's Allowance in 1985, 1998 and 2000, this report analyses the changing patterns of income deprivation that have occurred in this time period for different groups of people in England.

Paperback £15.95 ISBN 1 86134 409 0

Inequalities in life and death
What if Britain were more equal?

Richard Mitchell, Daniel Dorling and Mary Shaw
This follow up report to Death in Britain (Joseph Rowntree Foundation, 1997) – a study of changes in death inequalities from the 1950s to the 1990s – contains further evidence of the widening geographical gap in mortality in Britain, but shows how this gap might be narrowed through social and economic policies. The Death in Britain report claimed that Britain was failing to reach Target One of the World Health Organisation – to reduce inequalities in health by 2000. Inequalities in life and death provides conclusive evidence that Britain has failed to reach that target and argues that this failure need not continue.

Paperback £13.95 ISBN 1 86134 234 9

For further information about these and other titles published by The Policy Press, please visit our website at: www.policypress.org.uk or telephone +44 (0)117 954 6800
To order, please contact:
Marston Book Services
PO Box 269
Abingdon
Oxon OX14 4YN
UK Tel: +44 (0)1235 465500
Fax: +44 (0)1235 465556
E-mail: direct.orders@marston.co.uk